My Tummy Hurts

Junior Medical Detective Series

Kaushal Shah & Ali Raja

Illustrated by
Zara Mathews & Mel Casipit

To our familes, for their love and support.

Naya is on the way to Mila's birthday party with her mom. They're driving in the car and taking Chase, their next-door neighbor.

At Mila's birthday party, Chase is still unhappy.
"My tummy still hurts," he says again.
"Hey, wait a sec! We're not in the car anymore, so you
can't still be carsick."

Mila's dad says, "Chase, I bet you're just hungry. Let's get you a sandwich and some ice cream cake. I'm sure you'll feel better after you eat!"

Naya notices that Chase doesn't finish his ice cream cake. He is still holding his stomach. "I feel sad for him," Naya thinks to herself.

She grabs Chase by the hand and says, "Come on, Chase. Let's go and play. I'll push you in the car." While holding his hand, Naya notices that it feels warm.

Naya is pushing Chase in the play car and the car goes over a few small rocks. "Ouch!" Chase cries out.

Naya wonders, "Why does it hurt Chase to go over tiny bumps?" Chase is now holding the right side of his belly.

"Uh oh! Chase looks like he is going to throw up!

Eww!"

Another mom says, "Maybe he ate too much ice cream."
Someone's dad says, "It's probably just food poisoning."
"He probably just needs a nap. Let's take him home," says
Naya's mom.

Naya spreads her arms and shouts, "Hey, wait a sec! Chase didn't finish his ice cream, so we know that he didn't eat too much."

"And we all ate the same food and no one else is sick,
so we know it can't be food poisoning."
Everyone has stopped and is looking at her in surprise
with their mouths open.

Naya's mom says, feeling proud, "Naya, what would we do without you?

You saw so many things we didn't notice! Let's call his mom and dad and go to the hospital."

Chase is examined by a nurse and a doctor in the emergency room.
The nice nurse gives him some medicine that helps with the pain.

The doctor talks to Chase about how he feels, checks his tummy, and asks him if she can do an ultrasound.

The ultrasound shows a swollen appendix.
The doctor says, "Just what I thought -- appendicitis!"

The surgeon talks to Chase and his parents and says that Chase needs surgery.
"Thanks to you, he should be just fine," the surgeon says to Naya.

After Chase has his appendix removed, he says, "I want to finish my ice cream cake!" Everyone laughs!

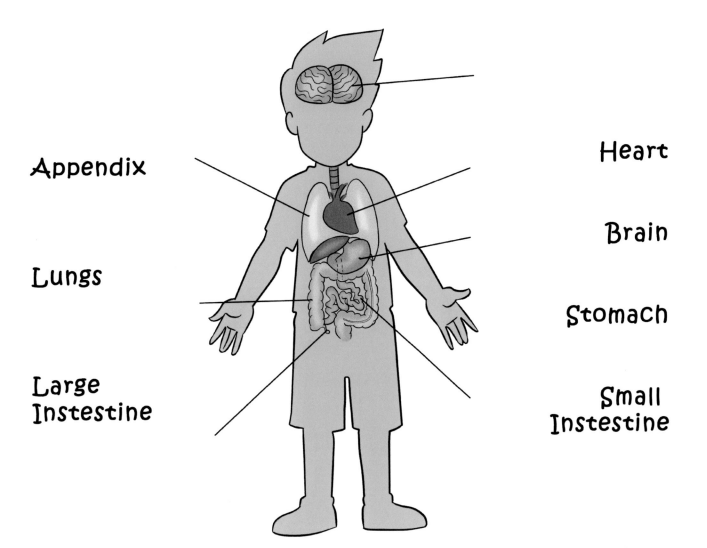

Appendix

Heart

Lungs

Brain

Large
Instestine

Stomach

Small
Instestine

Label the body parts!

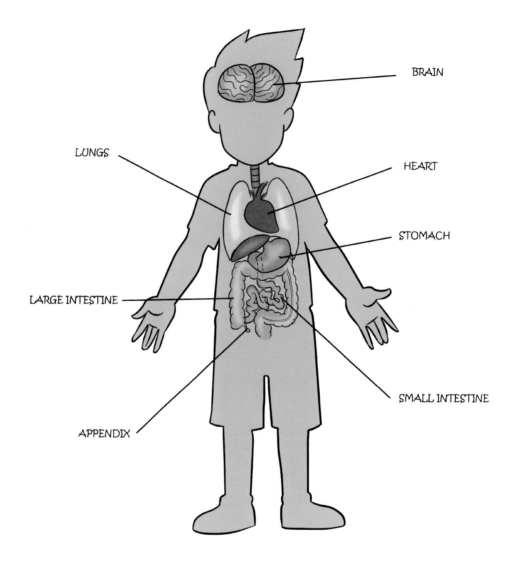

BRAIN

LUNGS

HEART

STOMACH

LARGE INTESTINE

SMALL INTESTINE

APPENDIX

Appendicitis: A swelling of the appendix, which is usually treated with medicine or surgery. Kids who have appendicitis usually have belly pain, vomiting, and fever – which you won't forget now that you've heard about Chase's story!

My Tummy Hurts

Junior Medical Detective Series

Kaushal Shah is an emergency physician in NYC who believes there is a medical detective in all of us -- you just have to learn to see the clues. He lives on Long Island with his wife, Vanisha, and their two mischievous daughters.

Ali Raja is an emergency physician in Boston. His son Chase has never had appendicitis but, if he gets it, Ali and his wife Danielle hope that his little brother Carter is able to diagnose it.

Zara Mathews is an emergency physician in New York, soon to be California. She credits her fiancé Arun, her parents Abe & Becky, and her brother Alex for always encouraging her to pursue her lifelong loves of both science and art.

Mel Casipit is an artist based in the Philippines. He is an Education graduate from Pangasinan State University. He does caricatures, illustrations and animation.

IN BOOK 2 OF THE JUNIOR MEDICAL DETECTIVE SERIES, THE GANG IS
GOING ON VACATION AND CARTER DOESN'T FEEL WELL AFTER HE IS
BITTEN BY A TICK. CAN NAYA, CHASE, AND MILA PUT THEIR HEADS
TOGETHER TO HIT THE BULLS-EYE WITH THEIR DIAGNOSIS?

Made in the USA
Middletown, DE
17 September 2017